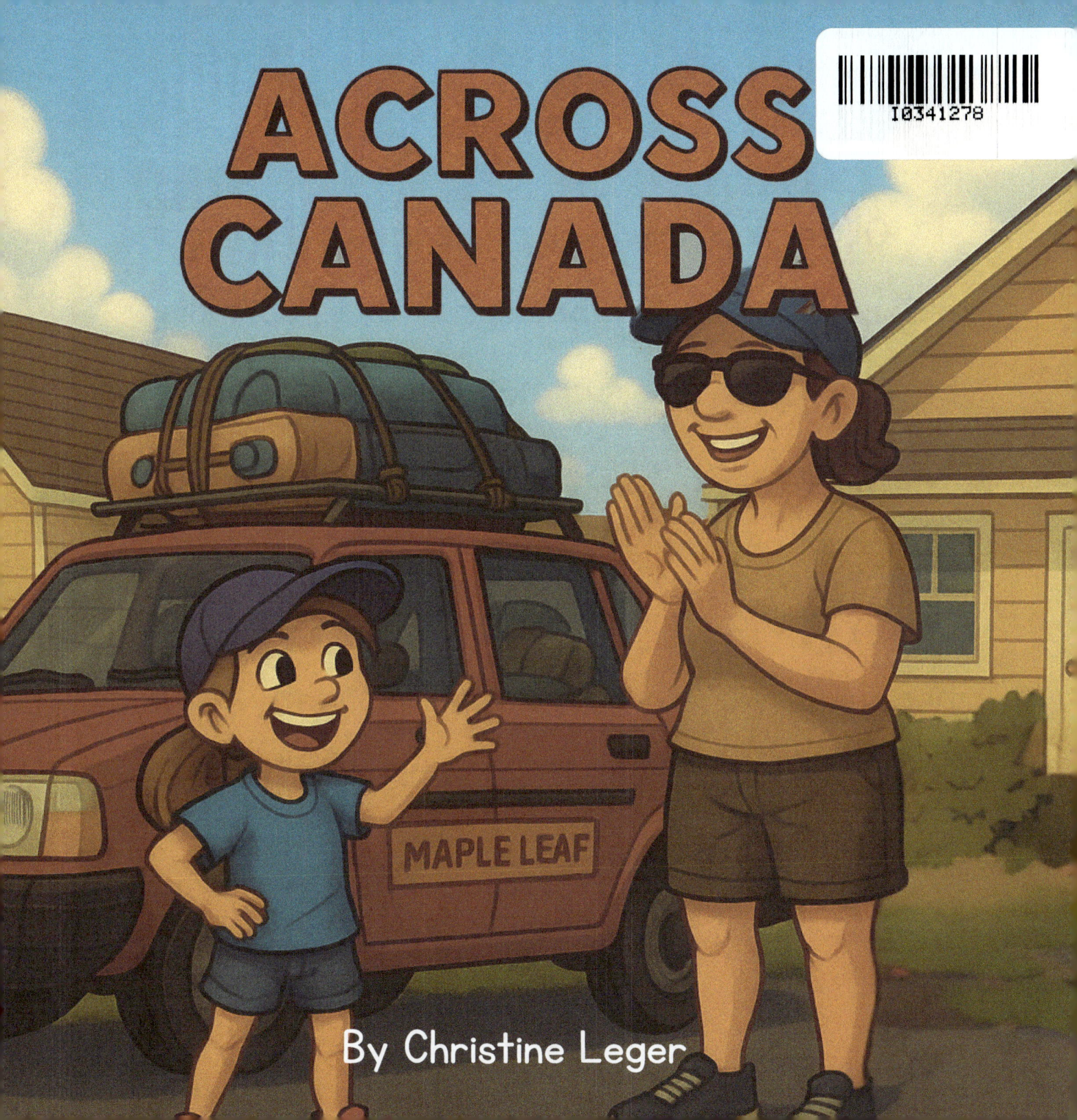

Olivia, a whirlwind of energy at ten years old, bounced on her heels, her eyes sparkling brighter than the summer sun. "Mémère, Mémère! Are we really doing this? Across Canada? Seriously?" Mémère Linda, her hair neatly pulled back and a mischievous twinkle in her own eyes, chuckled. "Seriously, my dear. Nova Scotia to British Columbia and back! A coast-to-coast adventure!"

Olivia had dreamt of this for years. She'd pored over maps, tracing routes with her finger, imagining towering mountains and endless prairies. And Mémère Linda, a woman with a spirit as vast as the Canadian landscape itself, had agreed to make that dream a reality. They were hitting every province, experiencing everything, and Olivia couldn't contain her excitement.

"Okay, Operation Maple Leaf is a go!" Mémère Linda announced, clapping her hands together. The "Maple Leaf," as they affectionately called their trusty, slightly-aged Volvo station wagon, was packed to the brim. Essentials included a cooler full of snacks (Olivia's favorite: Nanaimo bars), a first-aid kit, and a well-stocked emergency kit.

Olivia hopped into the back seat, surrounded by travel pillows and her favourite stuffed animals.

"Are we there yet?" she asked with a grin, mimicking the age-old travel complaint.

Mémère Linda laughed. "Not quite, sweetie. But the adventure begins now!"

Their journey started in Nova Scotia. Their first stop was Peggy's Cove, the iconic lighthouse standing sentinel against the crashing waves. Olivia collected a smooth, grey stone from the beach, declaring it her "Nova Scotia souvenir."

Then, they drove the breathtaking Cabot Trail on Cape Breton Island. The winding road, clinging to cliffs overlooking the endless ocean, stole Olivia's breath away. "Wow, Mémère," she whispered, "It's like the ocean goes on forever!"

As they crossed into New Brunswick, the anticipation grew. Their goal: whale watching! After a bumpy boat ride, Olivia squealed with delight as a massive humpback whale breached the surface, its enormous tail spraying water into the air. It was a moment she knew she'd never forget.

Olivia and Mémère Linda explored the towering flowerpot rocks at Hopewell Rocks, laughing as they walked on the ocean floor, amazed by the power of the tides.

Prince Edward Island was next, accessible via the Confederation Bridge. Olivia was mesmerized by the sheer length of it. They spent two days exploring the island, visiting the Anne of Green Gables Museum and eating fresh seafood by the ocean.

The seemingly endless highways of Quebec beckoned. In Quebec City, they explored the historic Chateau Frontenac, marvelling at its grandeur. "It looks like a castle from a fairy tale!" Olivia exclaimed.

They indulged in poutine (a must, according to Mémère Linda) and Olivia even surprised herself by enjoying a savoury tourtière, a traditional meat pie.

Ontario arrived, bringing with it a change of scenery. They visited Ottawa and Toronto, where they explored museums and learned about Canadian history.

Niagara Falls was a roaring spectacle of nature's power. They took a boat tour that went right up to the base of the falls. Olivia shrieked with laughter as they got soaked by the mist.

On the road to Thunder Bay, they stopped to admire the Terry Fox Monument to learn more about the hometown hero, and Olivia was really moved by Terry's courage. Mémère smiled proudly at Olivia's empathy.

The prairies of Manitoba and Saskatchewan stretched out before them, an ocean of golden wheat fields under a vast, blue sky. They stopped at roadside attractions, learned about the history of the region.

Olivia was fascinated by the stories of the First Nations people and the early settlers. Today, she and Mémère were at a Métis powwow, a vibrant celebration filled with music, dancing, and the sharing of traditions.

The air hummed with the beat of a giant drum. Boom, boom, boom. "Listen, Olivia," she whispered. "The drum is the heartbeat of the land."

Olivia watched dancers swirling in circles, their brightly coloured ribbons and beadwork flashing in the sun. Each dance told a story. There was the Fancy Shawl dance, like butterflies fluttering on the wind, and the Jingle Dress dance, where the shiny metal cones on the dresses jingled like raindrops.

Alberta was a landscape of contrasts. First, they were surrounded by dinosaur fossils. Olivia felt like a real-life paleontologist.

Next up was Calgary and the Calgary Stampede! The city was a whirlwind of cowboys, cowgirls, and Stampede fever! Olivia was wide-eyed with excitement.

They watched the rodeo, ate mini donuts, and even learned how to lasso (Olivia wasn't very good at it, but she had fun trying!). Mémère Linda even bought a pair of cowboy boots!

That night, they sat around a campfire, listening to country music under the starry Alberta sky.

Then, they entered Banff National Park, where the majestic Rocky Mountains scraped the sky, their snow-capped peaks reflected in turquoise lakes. They hiked along trails, breathing in the crisp mountain air, and Olivia felt a sense of awe she couldn't quite articulate.

British Columbia, their initial destination, was everything Olivia had dreamed of and more. The towering mountains, the lush forests, the vibrant city of Vancouver - it was a feast for the senses. They were so happy to reach their destination.

"We made it, Olivia!" Mémère Linda said, her voice choked with emotion. They had reached the far western edge of the country. A wave of accomplishment washed over them both.

The journey back east was filled with more adventures, more discoveries, and even more souvenirs. Olivia's rock collection grew, along with a collection of postcards, keychains, and quirky trinkets. The Maple Leaf groaned under the weight of their treasures.

Along the way, Mémère Linda shared stories of her own travels, reminiscing about adventures she'd had as a young woman. Olivia listened, captivated, realizing that her grandmother was more than just a Mémère – she was an explorer, a storyteller, a kindred spirit.

	"You know, Olivia," Mémère Linda said one evening, sitting by a crackling campfire under a canopy of stars, "the best part of travelling isn't just seeing new places. It's about the people you meet and the memories you make. And it's about discovering things you never knew about yourself."

Their final destination was Newfoundland, a rugged island province with a unique charm. They explored St. John's, the oldest city in North America, and hiked along the dramatic coastline. Olivia was fascinated by the colourful houses the friendly locals with their distinctive accents.

As their epic journey drew to a close, a sense of gratitude and accomplishment filled them. They had crossed Canada, explored its diverse landscapes, and deepened their bond in ways they never imagined.

Back home in Nova Scotia, The Maple Leaf overflowing with souvenirs, Olivia and Mémère Linda sat on the porch, sipping lemonade.

"What was your favourite part of the trip, Mémère?" Olivia asked, swinging her legs.

Mémère Linda smiled. "Spending it with you, my dear. Every single moment."

Olivia grinned, her heart full. She knew that this adventure, this incredible journey across Canada, was just the beginning. They were a team, a pair of explorers, ready to take on the world. And she couldn't wait to see where they would go next.

Every kilometer they drove was a memory that couldn't be taken from either of them. A forever bond stronger than ever.

www.ingramcontent.com/pod-product-compliance
Lightning Source LLC
Chambersburg PA
CBHW060538010526
44119CB00052B/755